FERRARI

RED-HOT LEGEND

BY JAY SCHLEIFER

Crestwood House
New York

Maxwell Macmillan Canada
Toronto

Maxwell Macmillan International
New York   Oxford   Singapore   Sydney

To Laura

Crestwood House
Macmillan Publishing Company
866 Third Avenue
New York, NY 10022

Maxwell Macmillan Canada, Inc.
1200 Eglinton Avenue East
Suite 200
Don Mills, Ontario M3C 3N1

Macmillan Publishing Company is part of the Maxwell Communication
Group of Companies.

Designed by R Studio T

Printed in the United States of America

10 9 8 7 6 5 4 3 2 1

Library of Congress Cataloging-in-Publication Data

Schleifer, Jay.
Ferrari / by Jay Schleifer.
p. cm.—(Cool classics)
Summary: Discusses the history and the dynamics of the popular
Italian sports car.
ISBN 0-89686-700-5
1. Ferrari automobile—History—Juvenile literature.   2. Ferrari,
Enzo, 1898—Juvenile literature.   [1. Ferrari automobile.]
I. Title. II. Series.
TL215.F47S35 1992
629.222'2—dc20   91-21374
                                        CIP
                                        AC

CONTENTS

For more than 40 years Ferraris have been the kings of road and track.

 **MORNING RIDE**

You're at a test track near Maranello, Italy, the home of the Ferrari sports-car company. It's a summer morning and you wonder which will be hotter today—the sun above you or the red Italian racing car in front of you.

The car is a Ferrari F40. Even for a Ferrari it's something special, built to mark the company's 40th birthday.

Let's find out just how special "special" is.

Swing open the lightweight door. Drop into the formfitting seat. Hook up the racing seat belts.

Now look around you. Even though this car can cost up to a *million dollars*, there's not even a radio. You soon find out why. This monster machine makes its own kind of music.

With a push of an old-fashioned starter button, gears grind, valves vibrate, pistons pulse with power. It all happens just behind your right ear. That's because the engine is mounted in the middle of the car.

Now reach for the long, shiny shifter. Most gearboxes feel kind of rubbery; not the one in this Ferrari. There's a metal plate with six slots into which you push the stick. It goes in as solidly as a key into a lock. *Thunk.* First gear. Now . . . rev the engine, drop the clutch . . . and go.

The engine kicks into gear. Then the wide rear tires light up like smoke bombs as 478 stampeding Italian horses struggle to grip the road. Suddenly the tire traction clicks and you're launched like a solid rocket booster!

The road becomes a blurry tunnel as this king of the road roars toward its top speed of 201 mph! In your mind, Corvettes, Porsches and other "lesser" cars are left behind. This world is suddenly too fast for them.

Here come the curves. You hit the massive brakes. Suddenly you slow down like a Navy Tomcat slamming to the deck in a carrier landing.

Too soon, the ride is over and the factory guys are yelling in Italian for their car back. You could make believe you don't understand them. No, that wouldn't be right. It's time to return to earth.

"Ferrari."

Is it the Italian word for "incredible"? No, but it should be.

2 THE MAN BEHIND THE MACHINE

The Ferrari story is as much about a man as about a car company. The man is Enzo Ferrari. He founded the company, and until he died in 1987, he was its heart and soul.

Just like the automobile, young Enzo grew up in the early years of the 20th century. His father ran a metalwork business that serviced Italy's railroads, so Enzo was surrounded by motors and machines almost from birth. Some reports say his family actually owned a car, a rarity at the time.

When Enzo was ten his father took him to see his first motor race—a local event near the family's hometown. Racing cars of the time were smoke-belching monsters. They made more noise than speed. You took your life in your hands when you rode in one. But as Enzo watched the racers slip and slide on the dirt, something roared to life within him. "The race made a great impression on me," Ferrari wrote later in his life story.

Enzo Ferrari

Great impression, indeed.

Some 50 years and thousands of races later, he was able to amaze friends by reciting every detail of that first event he had seen. He remembered who won, who came in second and even that the winning speed was 74 mph.

By age 12 he'd decided that what he wanted most in the world was to be a racing driver. The Italian government had other plans for him. At age 18 Enzo was drafted to serve in World War I. But as soon as he could break free of the green army uniform, Enzo sought a life colored by Italian racing red.

Most of Enzo Ferrari's magical machines, like this racing 308, are painted Italian racing red.

In 1920, with the help of an ex-army buddy, he got a job test-driving cars for one of the car companies of the time. Enzo, of course, believed that there was no better way to test cars than to race them.

Driving first for a small Italian car company, and then for the more famous Alfa-Romeo, Enzo's racing career prospered. Racing in those days was more than a little wild and woolly. Drivers often traveled cross-country to races by driving in their own machines, battling their way through mud, snow, bad roads and even wild animals. On one trip Ferrari fought off a wolf attack, using a pistol he kept under the seat.

But driving wasn't Enzo's only talent. He'd begun managing Alfa's racing team. He seemed to know how to get the best from drivers and mechanics. He used humor, cleverness and, at times, a mighty volcano of a temper.

At this point Enzo Ferrari decided to field his own team of Alfa cars. That team soon became known as **Scuderia Ferrari**, "Ferrari's racing stable."

Every stable needs a horse and Enzo's soon had one—the famous Ferrari prancing horse symbol.

As Ferrari told the story later, he'd received the symbol from a rich countess whose son was a pilot in the war. The young man's plane had been shot down and the son was killed. But the mother had kept a piece of the airplane's frame, on which was painted the famous horse. "We entrust this to you," the mother wrote Ferrari. She meant it as a tribute to Enzo's bravery and spirit. Thereafter, the prancing black horse on a yellow shield would gallop across the nose of every Ferrari Enzo built.

The famous prancing horse emblem. It was a gift to Ferrari from the mother of a fighter pilot who died bravely in battle.

Scuderia Ferrari was successful from the day the team was formed. But Ferrari wanted more speed and power than the Alfa cars he used could provide. He then made the decision that marked a major turn in his life. He would build his own racing car. And he started the project immediately.

But by now it was 1940. World War II was about to consume Italy. Suddenly, bullets and bombs, not racing victories, overtook Enzo's life.

3 ONTO THE WORLD'S STAGE

The war was a disaster for Italy. Ruled by the dictator Benito Mussolini, Italy entered into a partnership with Adolf Hitler. Ultimately that partnership put Italy on the losing side of the war. Ferrari was against the war. His main interest was racing, and war got in the way of that. While waiting the war out, Enzo ran a small engine parts company near the city of Modena.

American bombers had something to say about that. Twice they dropped their deadly loads on the Ferrari factory. Germany, Italy's one-time ally, was no kinder. When Italy quit the war early, German forces stole Ferrari's machinery and goods and took them back to Germany. Through it all, Ferrari dreamed of one goal: completing his own race car.

When the war ended in mid-1945, he got his chance. Bringing together talented friends from his Alfa-Romeo days, Ferrari began to work again on the machine of his dreams.

Building a car from scratch isn't easy. Many have tried and failed. But Ferrari didn't simply want to build a car. He'd decided to build one of the most advanced cars in the world.

If there's a race there's a Ferrari in it. This open-wheeler competes in a class called Formula 2.

His dream began with the engine. The first decision was how many cylinders it should have. Most cars of the time had four or six cylinders. Some, mostly big American sedans, used eight. Ferrari announced to the car world that his new car would have *12* cylinders.

To Ferrari and his engine designer, a man named Columbo, the reasons went beyond pride and glory.

All car engines work by spraying a mist of gasoline and air into their **cylinders**. The mist is exploded with an electric spark. The force of the explosion drives a **piston**, which moves inside the cylinder. Passed through other parts, that motion finally turns the wheels.

The larger the cylinders, the more power the engine can generate. But big cylinders mean fat, slow-moving pistons. There's a limit to how fast the engine can turn. That saps speed.

By using 12 tiny cylinders instead of fewer, larger ones, Ferrari got power without using heavy pistons. His new engine could safely turn over at incredible speeds, up to 7,000 revolutions per minute. The engine he built was not very large. It was only about 1.5 liters—the same size you'd find in a smaller Toyota. But turning as fast as it did, the new Ferrari power plant generated up to three times the power of other engines of the same size.

There was another reason Enzo chose to build a "12." He loved the incredible shrieking sound of all those little sparkplug explosions going off. "It was like music," he said.

But more cylinders meant more spinning, whirring parts tearing at each other. This required a greater need for perfection. For a giant car company it would have been an engineering triumph to build a brand new 12 from scratch. For Ferrari and his tiny band of followers, working in war-torn Italy, it was close to a miracle.

The car they built was called the Ferrari 125 S.

From the day it left the tiny factory, the Ferrari showed its greatness. In its first race in May 1947, the car had both speed and staying power. When a small part went out two laps from the checkered flag, Ferrari's driver was well in the lead.

Their first win came just two weeks later. Many others followed. Within a year Ferraris were the cars to beat at races all over Europe. In the year 1949 alone this tiny three-year-old car company won 32 races, including the world's best-known sports-car event, the 24-hour race at Le Mans, France. Enzo Ferrari's fame spread. He had now become the supplier of cars to the stars, as well as being a superstar himself. Hardly a week would pass without a visit or call from a famous would-be buyer. Kings and princes ordered Ferraris. So did the rich from all walks of life.

Ferrari had more customers than he had cars. He could choose those he would "allow" to buy Ferrari cars. And plenty of the great names of the 1940s and 1950s had to wait endlessly in the tiny showroom of the factory for **"Il Commendatore"** ("The Boss") to see them.

✝In his little empire of speed and glory, Enzo Ferrari was king. He'd even begun signing his letters with royal purple ink. But it was the royal performance of his cars that kept this king on his throne.

4 THE BEAUTIFUL BARCHETTA

If the 125 S boosted Ferrari's fame off the ground, his next car put it into orbit. The factory called it the Model 166 MM. Everyone else in the sports-car world took a look at its clean, speedboatlike lines and called it "**Barchetta**" ("Little Boat").

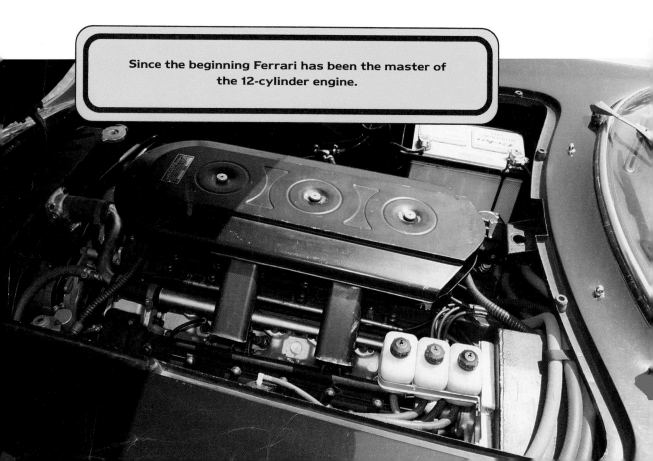

Since the beginning Ferrari has been the master of the 12-cylinder engine.

Like the 125 S, the heart of the Barchetta was the Ferrari V-12 engine. Though it only produced about 125 horsepower, that was plenty of power to move a car that weighed only about three-fourths of a ton. "Hit the starter button and it's instant action," wrote one Barchetta driver. "That tiny V-12, with its lightweight parts, can spin to amazing power before you have time to react."

But unlike the heavy-looking 125 S, the looks of the Barchetta were light and clean. The car seemed to float over the road with perfect grace. Most Ferrari fans agree it was one of the prettiest sports cars ever built. The factory still gets letters asking that they produce a modern version of it.

Barchettas were built for both racing and street use. There wasn't much difference between the two. The street version had about the same weather protection for the driver—meaning just about none, not even a top. The street machine's body was also built of the same lightweight **aluminum** as the racer's. The aluminum was so easy to bend that an innocent passerby might dent it just by leaning on it!

Despite its drawbacks, the Barchetta gave its drivers something really special. They got the same feeling driving down a New York street or a California freeway that racing drivers got tearing past the grandstands at Le Mans.

 5 **THE BIGGER, THE BETTER**

The first Ferrari V-12 was an incredible engine. But by 1950 it no longer had enough power to win at the racetrack. Ferrari's rivals, including Alfa-Romeo, had caught up by building more powerful engines. Ferrari needed something better.

That something better turned out to be bigger as well. Ferrari designers took the basic V-12 design and enlarged it. Where the original engine had measured only 1.5 liters, the new one started out at 3.3 liters and moved up from there. In time it was over 4 liters.

The result was a major increase in horsepower. The old design generated about 125 horses under the hood. The new engines pumped more than 300!

As power rose, performance skyrocketed! Top speeds, which were never more than 140 mph with the "little" V-12, now zoomed to over 180.

The new engine was installed in several different models. But the one many remember best is called the 375 Plus. The Plus has been described as "all engine, with only enough car to hold the engine off the road." The car had so much power for its weight that even expert drivers had trouble controlling it. |

 **COMING TO AMERICA**

The early 1950s marked Ferrari's one and only try at the famous Indianapolis 500 race. While few Americans had ever heard of Le Mans, everyone knew the Indy. A win there would make Ferrari as famous in the States as he was becoming in the rest of the racing world.

Ferrari gave it a shot. Arriving at Indianapolis in 1952, the Boss brought one of his fastest racers. This red open-wheeler was simply called the "Ferrari Special."

Part of what made it special was the driver—the great Alberto Ascari. With some 400 horsepower under his right foot, Ascari lapped the famous brick oval faster and faster with each practice mile.

At first, American drivers scoffed at the fellow with the "funny" accent in car number 12. But as time passed, some began to believe that this talented foreigner might have a chance to win "America's Race."

On race day the Ferrari took its place among the 33 fire-breathing machines picking up speed behind the pace car. At the green flag, which started the race, Ascari surged through the pack. But soon he began to feel a sickening wobble in one of the wheels. The wire spokes between the rim and hub had weakened. Soon after, the wheel collapsed in a heap. Ascari skidded off the track. He was unhurt, but done for the day.

As it turned out, Ferrari was done with Indy for good. Although Enzo promised year in and year out that he would someday capture the great American prize, he never came back.

Though finished with Indy, Ferrari was far from finished with America. In fact, he had just started.

Enzo's American connection was a man named Luigi Chinetti. Chinetti, a race driver, car dealer and longtime friend, believed that the Ferraris could sell in the United States. At first Enzo disagreed, but Chinetti kept bothering his old friend to give it a try.

Finally Ferrari told him, "If you buy five, I'll let you sell in America." Chinetti bought 20. He quickly sold them all.

In time, Ferrari began to build special models for buyers in the United States. American superhighways were ideal for high-speed cruising, so the specials were built with long, rapid trips in mind. They tended to be bigger than cars made for Europe. These were sleek road-rockets, made to cross whole states at bullet speed.

In the state of Nevada there were no speed limits on its highways. Legally you could go as fast as you wanted to. But this was before gasoline became high-priced and sometimes hard to get. It wasn't unusual to find sleek red "America" model Ferraris (that's what they were called) streaking across the desert at 150 mph.

In time, the company came up with even higher-powered versions called "Superamerica" models. And because Ferraris sold especially well on the West Coast, there was a special "California" model.

The America and California were typical of big touring Ferraris of the 1950s. Their V-12 engines were technologically complex for the times, but the rest of the car was almost go-cart simple. The front-mounted engine drove the rear wheels. The frame was made of straight metal tubes. **Suspension** was almost as simple as horse-and-wagon designs. And long after other cars began installing modern **disk brakes**, Ferrari still used an old-fashioned drum design.

Yet when Ferrari's parts were bolted together, a kind of magic took place. Especially in the 250 GTO.

⬡7 THE UNFORGETTABLE GTO

In America in the early 1960s General Motors Corporation, the maker of the Pontiac, was trying to change its image among buyers. For years Pontiacs had been seen as slow and dull. Now General Motors decided Pontiac would be the "hot" GM name-plate. Or, as the company's ads later put it, "We build excitement!"

The makers of the Pontiac created a fast new model—the fastest car they'd ever sold. The car was called the Pontiac GTO.

GM didn't invent the name. They borrowed it from Ferrari. At least they borrowed from the best. Many Ferrari lovers think the Ferrari 250 GTO was the finest Ferrari ever.

Like many Ferraris before it, the 250 GTO had its roots in racing. **17**

The top-selling Ferraris of the 1950s came from the 250 series.

It had long been a dream among sports-car lovers to own a car they could race on Sunday and then drive to work on Monday.

The Barchetta was a car like that. But during the 1950s racing cars, Ferraris included, had become more and more specialized. They were costly, high-strung thoroughbreds useful on the racetrack only.

To change that, race officials announced a new set of rules for the world's sports-car championship. Cars raced had to be legally driveable on the street. They had to have two seats, usable lights and full weather protection. Such cars were called "Gran Turismo" or "GT" cars.

The rules further stated that a factory had to build at least 100 copies of anything it raced in the sports-car competitions. As no team needed that many cars, the 100 copy rule assured that the hot new car really would be offered for sale to the public.

To prove they had followed the rules, factories had to file official papers. The Italian term for this is *omologato*. When it was approved for racing, the GT car then became known as a **GTO**— *Gran Turismo Omologato*.

At the time, Ferrari was building a beautiful street machine called the 250. It was fast, but not a racer. By making certain changes to the 250, Enzo Ferrari felt he could produce a car as strong on the track as it was on the road.

Enzo began by removing the street car's V-12 engine. In its place he put a much more highly tuned engine from one of the racing Ferraris. This upped horsepower from about 300 to almost 400.

Now he turned his attention to the body. The 250 was a lovely car, but rather squarish in shape. Ferrari felt the car would be faster if it were more streamlined. Designers added a low, sharklike nose and made the tail longer, ending it in a little upward wing shape. They also cut holes in the body to help cool the super-hot engine.

Then to check their new look, the designers tried something seldom done before. They took their car to a **wind tunnel**, a testing device used in developing the shape of aircraft.

The tunnel blew a blast of air over the GTO's body shape at **19**

Another 250 series car was the 250 LM, designed to run at Le Mans. This was among the first midengine Ferraris.

speeds of up to 200 mph. When puffs of smoke were introduced into the windstream, designers could clearly see how air traveled over the body. Anything that slowed the flow of air could be instantly smoothed out. These days, almost all auto designs are checked in a wind tunnel. The GTO was among the first tested this way.

The car was now shaped right, and had power to match. To reduce speed-robbing weight, Enzo next turned to the 250's interior. Everything not required came out.

Anyone who's ever sat in a GTO is amazed that Ferrari could say that this was anything but a racer. The car has almost no noiseproofing. It has only the barest seat padding, and all the windows except the windshield are made of plastic, not glass.

If the driver had it rough, the passenger had it even rougher. He or she had to share the seat with the battery, a frame tube and an oil tank. The tank gets uncomfortably hot when the motor is running.

All the changes added up to one thing: performance. The GTO is one of the fastest Ferrari two-seaters ever built, with great handling and a top speed upward of 170 mph.

No plush cushions or fuzzy dice! In a Ferrari, the driver's "office" is all business.

Race results were spectacular. GTOs won the new racing class hands down, winning the world's GT championship in the car's first year.

Among all Ferraris, the GTO is one of the rarest. Only 39 were built, and if you want to buy one today, you'll have to get a collector to part with it. The price is likely to be over two million dollars!

What happened to the rule that said Ferrari had to build 100 copies of his new race car, not 39?

Ferrari simply told officials that his new supercar was just a slightly changed 250. And he'd built many more than 100 of those.

8 THE WAR AGAINST FORD

Everyone knows the story of David and Goliath. In the tale a boy takes on a giant of great size and strength and wins the battle with brainpower and bravery over brawn.

A real-life David and Goliath story happened in auto racing in the mid-1960s. Ferrari played the part of David. Playing Goliath was no less than the gigantic Ford Motor Company.

During those years, Ford decided it would be good for car sales if their vehicles had a sporty image. They took many steps toward this goal. First, Ford sedans were crammed bumper to bumper with hot-rod parts. Some ran in **NASCAR** stock car races. Then the company got together with sports-car builder Caroll Shelby to create a new supercar. Ford supplied the engines, Shelby supplied the rest. The result was the famous Shelby Cobra.

And of course, Ford built the Mustang—the world's first popular-priced sporty car.

But the head of the company, Henry Ford II, wanted more. Mr.

Ford's challenge to Ferrari began with the famous
Cobra, a combination of an English body and a Ford
V-8 engine.

Ford, one of the world's most powerful men, had a great love of European sports-car racing. He knew that the crown jewel of racing was the 24 Hours of Le Mans. He decided he wanted a Ford to win at Le Mans.

It didn't matter that Ford had never entered a major sports-car event. Or that they had neither a racing car nor had even an idea for a car. With more than 100,000 employees and billions of dollars at his fingertips, Mr. Ford would get what he wanted. It was as simple as that.

Once their boss's wishes were known, Henry's assistants tried to come up with a plan to carry them out.

The answer seemed simple. With the money Ford Motor had to play with, they'd simply *buy* a car company that knew how to win at Le Mans. And wasn't there such a company somewhere in Italy? The name started with an F. Whatever price Enzo wanted, Ford had the money to pay.

A meeting with Ferrari was arranged and Ford men were quickly on their way to Maranello, Italy. We know what the results of the meeting were. And we can easily imagine what it was like:

Picture Enzo Ferrari sitting behind his big desk, his great head of white hair like the mane of a lion, his stony face like that of a Roman emperor. He might even be wearing his trademark sunglasses, which he often wore indoors.

Ferrari listens carefully to the men in gray suits from Detroit. The price is right. And Ferrari had been thinking of selling part of his company so he can spend more time on his beloved racing. Hmmm, Enzo thinks, perhaps this is possible after all.

Then the head of the Ford group makes the big mistake.

"And so, Signore [Mr.] Ferrari, in the new company, the cars will no longer be called 'Ferraris.' They'll be 'Ferrari-Fords.'"

The great man says nothing for a time, but his face is turning as red as one of his cars. Inside, of course, Ferrari's famous temper is rising like hot lava in one of Italy's ancient volcanoes.

"What?" he shouts, his voice as shrill as a V-12. "These are Ferraris and only Ferraris! Out! Get out!" The Ford men leave but they can't understand why he's so angry. After all, in the new name of the car, they did offer to put his name *first*.

When Henry Ford heard Ferrari's reaction, it was his turn to have a tantrum. Mr. Ford didn't care what it cost or what his company had to do. "Beat Ferrari," he ordered his men.

The Great Ferrari-Ford War was on.

In any war the side with the best weapons has the best chance to win. Ferrari had a talented group of racing specialists. The cars they'd designed had by this time won thousands of races, including Le Mans. But they were few in number—about 70 workers. And the money they had was a tiny part of what Ford had to spend.

Ford took care of its biggest problem—no car—quickly. Ferrari had not been willing to sell out, but an English race-car company named Lola was. Within a few weeks, they had a hot design that could only get better the more they worked on it. They soon redesigned the English machine into an American supercar called the Ford GT-40.

The problem was that Le Mans was coming up in just a few months. Ford broke speed records to get ready, but the GT-40 had many bugs still to work out. The two Fords that entered broke down, and Ferrari easily won the 1964 Le Mans race.

But as his team cheered the victory, Enzo Ferrari must have felt uneasy. He knew that Ford would be back.

For 1965 Ford did return, with a group of better-developed cars. But as the race droned on, Ford after Ford dropped out. When the finish came at four o'clock on a Sunday afternoon, a Ferrari had again crossed the finish line first.

With the creation of the fabulous Ford GT-40, the
Ferrari-Ford fight turned into a racing war!

It wasn't even the latest model Ferrari, but one from a few years
before.

This made Henry Ford even madder. In 1966 his team didn't just
race at Le Mans, they waged total war. The Ford team showed up
with 13 cars against the four-car Ferrari factory team. And what
cars the Fords were! The Americans had ripped out the GT-40's
original engine, which was about the same size as Ferrari's. In its
place they bolted in the monster V-8 used in Ford's NASCAR
racers. Its cylinders were a full seven liters—twice the size of those
in the Ferrari V-12. It was the biggest racing engine many at Le
Mans had ever seen!

As the racers roared off, many Ferrari fans felt that this time their hero had no chance at all. But once again, Ford after Ford dropped out, and Ferrari hopes began to rise.

But the killer race was just as hard on the Italian as on the American cars. As day turned to night, the Ferraris began to die. And when dawn broke, there was nothing left of Enzo's team. Only three of the 13 Fords survived, but that was enough. They finished 1–2–3.

Henry Ford finally got his win at Le Mans. But it had taken four years, millions of dollars and the hard work of a worldwide team to finally beat Enzo Ferrari.

To prove that his win was more than just luck, Ford sent his team back in 1967 and won again. Fords also took the race in 1968 and 1969, for four straight wins.

But in this David and Goliath story, did the giant really win?

Ask anyone who knows automobiles to name the company that builds some of the world's most exciting cars. Or to tell you what car name means the most in auto racing glory. Chances are that the name they come up with will begin with an "F." And end with an "i."

9 THE DYNAMITE DAYTONA

If the war with Ford taught Enzo Ferrari anything, it was the value of a great, big engine. As the 1960s ended, Enzo decided to put this lesson to work in a brand new road car.

He had other reasons for offering a new Ferrari for sale. Enzo was not the only Italian building great-looking supercars. Companies like Alfa-Romeo and Maserati had been around for years. And a hot new company had been started by, of all people, a farm

27

Mounting the engine in the middle balances the car's weight for better handling.

tractor maker. The man's name was Ferrucio Lamborghini.

"Lambo" had started out building a car much like Ferrari's. The engine was a V-12, mounted up front. But the company soon switched to mounting their engine in the middle of the car. This balanced the car's heaviest parts between front and rear, improving handling. Race cars, including Ferrari's, had used this design for years. But Lamborghini was among the first to put it in their street machines.

This machine was a winged beauty that was more airplane than auto—the new Lamborghini Countach. Even its name was exciting. *Countach* means "wow" in Italian.

When the new midengine Lambos rolled out, reporters rushed to get Enzo Ferrari's views. Would the next Ferrari have a midmounted engine? they wanted to know.

Enzo had the perfect answer: "The horse pulls the cart, he does not push it." His cars would keep the engines in the front.

Ferrari had more than an answer, though. He was about to introduce the last great front-engine Ferrari. The factory called the car the 365 GTB/4. Everybody else called it the Daytona, after the famous American racetrack.

The greatness of the Daytona began with its styling. The Daytona's **designer**, a man named Pininfarina, had created many Ferraris. But for the Daytona he came up with a whole new look.

The car was rounded, yet sharp-edged. The headlights were hidden for a more streamlined shape. The hood was two-thirds of the car, as if the engine was all that mattered—which wasn't far from the truth at Ferrari.

The Daytona was so stunning it quickly inspired other car-makers. Compare it to the original Datsun 240Z, one of the most popular sports cars of the 1970s. What you see resembles a mini-Ferrari Daytona.

But the new Ferrari's beauty was more than skin-deep. Within that skin lived the mighty new four-liter V-12. Punching out more than 350 horsepower, this was one power plant that never ran out of power. "This car only begins to come alive over 70 mph," said one driver. "And at 140, it's not even breathing hard. This baby is designed for perfect control at 174 mph."

The last Daytona rolled from the Ferrari plant in 1973. About 1,300 were built in all.

Ferrari's best designs were created by a car builder named Pininfarina. They're rounded, but they sure look sharp!

If you want a Daytona today you'd have to buy one from a collector at a cost of around a million dollars. But if you just want a car that *looks* like a Daytona, that's easier. A small company in Florida removes the body from late-model Corvettes. They then pop on a **fiberglass** shell that looks just like Ferrari's finest. Such a car was used in TV's "Miami Vice" police show a few years ago. It was seen every week—until in one story the bad guys blew it sky-high with explosives. (A real Daytona would have been too valuable to destroy.)

The Ferrari Daytona. What a dynamite car!

10 "FERRARI'S CHEVROLET"

When most people think of Ferrari, they think of V-12 engines. The Italian builder put a V-12 in his first car and in many of his greatest cars. But he was too good an **engineer** not to try another kind of engine. Over the years, there have been Ferrari V-8s, V-6s and, believe it or not, even four-cylinder cars.

Many of these "baby" Ferrari power plants were created by Ferrari's son Alfredino. "Dino," as everyone called him, worked side by side with his famous father in the early 1950s. Then, in 1956 a tragic road test accident took his life. Dino was only in his 20s.

Dino's death hit Enzo Ferrari hard. For years the great man could not bring himself to speak openly about it. And he made sure fresh flowers were always delivered to the young man's grave. But he also honored his beloved son in another way. Ferrari decided to build a car with a V-6 engine, a design Dino favored as much as Enzo loved the V-12.

The car first appeared at a 1956 auto show. The new car was

The V-6 powered Dino was named after Ferrari's son.

stunning, low and sleek. And it had something even the big V-12s didn't have—a midmounted engine.

Although the car looked like a Ferrari, the Ferrari name and the famous prancing horse emblem were nowhere to be seen. Enzo had given the car a new name, one to honor his son: the Dino 206.

In the next few years more Dino models followed. Though not as fast as the big machines, they didn't cost as much either. This made the car very popular.

To help build Dinos, Ferrari had put together a deal with a giant Italian car company, Fiat. With the factories of Fiat on the team, thousands of Dinos could be built.

This was the closest Enzo Ferrari would ever get to building a car for "all the people." The Dino was "Ferrari's Chevrolet."

By 1976 Dino models had switched from a V-6 to a V-8 engine, giving them more power and speed. Something else was switched too: The car now carried the Ferrari name.

In the last few years most Ferraris built have been the Dino type, with midmounted V-8 engines. Such popular models as the 308, 328 (the car driven by Tom Selleck in TV's "Magnum P.I.") and the 348 can all be traced to the design Enzo's son started.

The 308 is one of the most popular recent models. Tom Selleck drove a similar car in TV's "Magnum, P.I."

THE BOXERS ENTER THE RING

For years, Enzo had fought the idea of building a midengine 12-cylinder road car. (The Dinos were sixes and eights.) When his rivals at Lamborghini built midengine 12s, Ferrari made jokes about them.

All the while, though, Ferrari was at work on a midengine 12. But it was *his* kind of midengine 12.

The car finally went on sale in the early 1970s, and it was a stunner—with a highly unusual name: The "**Boxer.**"

For the Boxer, Ferrari had created an entirely new kind of 12-cylinder engine—a "flat 12." His rivals used the V-12 layout in their cars.

If you look at the letter V you'll notice how tall it is. V-layout engines are tall too. In a front-engine car that's not a problem. Builders set the engine low between the front wheels.

But the middle of a car is crowded with other parts. So the car needs to be made longer. Then those parts can be moved to make room for the engine. The problem is that a longer car is usually a clumsier car.

To solve all this, Enzo built his engine flat, like a pancake.

Like the V-12s, it had six cylinders on each side. But the cylinders lay flat, pointed toward each other. The pistons inside seemed to jab toward each other, like two fighters throwing punches, hence the name "Boxer."

With a flat-12, Ferrari could build a shorter, lower car. That translated into super performance.

The Boxer was incredibly fast. Its top speed was 188 mph, 15 mph faster than the Daytona, Ferrari's best front-engine car. A Boxer

The "Boxer" featured a V-12 engine in which the pistons moved toward each other. Its top speed was 180 mph!

could jump from zero to 60 mph in less than six seconds and reach 100 mph in 12 seconds. Handling was fabulous too.

Magazine writers who test-drove the car found themselves writing out of control with praise. "The sound is a fierce bark like a racing engine," wrote one expert, "that's followed by an awesome wail that comes from enormous strength."

Another writer gushed about the car's ability to get up and go:

"Step on it from a standing start and you get one long, staggering push forward. Unbelievably fast!"

But not unbelievably perfect, as it turned out. The Boxer had one little problem: It wanted to fly!

At high speed the front end would actually lift slightly off the ground. This is good for an airplane, but not for a car. A car needs its tires to grip the ground.

"Just keep the speed down a little," said one expert, "and any drive is a joy."

For all their speed and looks Boxers were not very comfortable. The interior was cramped and hard to get in and out of. What's more, Ferrari left part of the car's cooling system in front even though he'd moved the engine to the middle. That meant hot water and oil pipes from the engine passed right through the passenger area.

The Boxer was toasty warm in the winter. But it was toasty warm in the summer too!

The Boxer was never sold in the United States. Ferrari decided he didn't want to make changes to the car to pass U.S. safety and pollution laws. Perhaps one reason was that he knew there would soon be an even more incredible midengine Ferrari.

(12) THE TERRIFIC TESTAROSSA

When word came out that there would soon be a new top-of-the-line Ferrari, the auto world thought it knew what to expect.

For years Enzo's machines had featured stunning looks and staggering go-power. But they also had their flaws. Most weren't very roomy, nor richly made for what they cost. They had no real luggage room to speak of. And as for quality control, parts from one side of early-model Ferraris sometimes measured differently from the matching parts on the other side. Ferrari lovers figured all this was the price you had to pay for fun—and they expected more of the same in the new car.

They were in for a major surprise.

The new Ferrari was called the "**Testarossa**," which in Italian means "Red Head." It was named after a racing car of the 1950s, and also because the top of the engine cylinder heads were painted bright red.

As it sat on a showroom turntable collecting stares and envy, the new Testarossa was wildly different from anything people had seen before.

Or perhaps we should say it was *widely* different.

A minitruck in size from left to right, the Testarossa stretched more than six and a half feet across from taillight to taillight. That was half a foot wider than the Boxer, and even wider than a

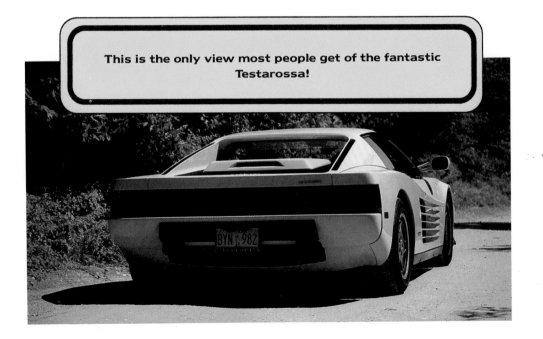

This is the only view most people get of the fantastic Testarossa!

Chevrolet Corvette. The "TR," as many called it, was also longer than the Boxer.

There was a reason for all this size. Ferrari had built the most comfortable car the company had ever put on the road. Even six-foot-tall drivers could spread their elbows, stretch their legs and have all the room they needed for a fun time at the wheel.

The company had done something about the Boxer's problem of hot pipes under the seats too. The engine's cooling units had been moved from the front to the sides of the car. Cool air entered through giant vents at the sides and exited out the back. The engine stayed cool, the passengers were cooler and the vents looked incredible. They created a side view that no other car could match.

Even the rearview mirror turned heads as it went by. It was mounted on long stalklike supports so the driver could see out behind the wide rear body. And the mirror seemed to fly alongside the car.

For all its new looks and comfort the Testarossa lost nothing in performance. In fact it gained. The TR engine pumped nearly 400 horsepower. Sixty mph came and went in under five seconds. And top speed was better than 180.

The Boxer pulled similar numbers. But the TR did it with a lot more luxury and class.

Unlike some earlier Ferraris, the TR was built right! Parts fit and worked. Switches switched. Lights lit. The air conditioner pumped a storm of cool air even on the hottest days. Veteran Ferrari drivers thought they'd died and gone to heaven.

What really happened was an important change at Ferrari. Through much of the company's history, Ferraris were handbuilt. But even the finest craftsmen make mistakes.

For the Testarossa Ferrari installed new, high-tech machines that did their jobs right time after time. They worked more quickly too, allowing Ferrari to build greater numbers of cars than ever before. Thousands, instead of dozens or hundreds, could be built.

The little factory in Maranello wasn't likely to outbuild General Motors. But it was becoming a more competitive car company. After all, the Ferrari company was nearly 40 years old, and getting ready for the 21st century.

Meanwhile, Enzo Ferrari was nearly 90, and in poor health. Everyone honored him, but few felt he would ever again have much to do with the cars his company built.

Not so. Before he died Enzo Ferrari had one more masterpiece to give to the world.

This view of the Testarossa shows how wide it is . . . more than six feet between the headlights.

 **F40: THE WILDEST FERRARI OF ALL!**

Through his long life, Enzo Ferrari's greatest love was auto racing. Ferrari cars have won between 4,000 and 5,000 races, a record unmatched by any other nameplate.

Maybe it's as it should be, then, that Enzo's last and greatest car began life as a racer. The car didn't have a name. It was called simply the F40.

Where did the F40 come from?

Ferraris can get really wild. This special racing BB model previewed the high rear wing of the F40.

In the early 1980s racing officials announced a new world's championship called Group B. As in the days of the old GTO, Group B cars were to be racers that also ran on the street. But all sorts of high-tech engineering was allowed.

Group B racing promised to be fast and furious—exactly the kind Enzo enjoyed. So he set his people to the task of building a Group B car.

But officials had a change of heart about the new racing series. They decided that the new "Killer Bs," as people called them, might be too fast and dangerous to be raced. Group B was canceled after just a few races.

That left Ferrari with a racing car, but no races in which to run it.

But the crafty old master of performance cars knew exactly what to do.

The company's 40th birthday was coming up. That was reason for a special car. Enzo decreed that the new car be a "king of the hill" Ferrari. It would be the fastest, highest-performance car the company had ever created.

It was decided that the car would be called F40 to honor the birthday, and that it would be based on the Group B design.

On July 21, 1987, Enzo Ferrari stood at the center of his factory beside a covered red object. As reporters took notes, the most famous man in racing began to speak.

"A year ago, I gave my engineers a task. It was to build a car that was to be the best in the world. And now it is here." As the cloth was dramatically swept aside, the world saw the F40 for the first time.

What it saw was a ground-hugging road shark that looked like it ate lesser cars for snacks. The nose nearly touched the ground at one end while a high tail split the air at the other.

Front and rear wheels were of different sizes. The front ones were the perfect size for steering, the rear for traction. There was no spare tire of either size. Maybe Enzo figured anyone who could afford an F40 could afford towing.

The gleaming red paint job hid the fact that the body was partly made of space-age materials called **composites**. They were lighter yet stronger than either steel or fiberglass. The same type of materials are used in the F-14, F-16 and F-18 jet fighters!

One look inside told you that this car was built for ultimate performance, and not much else. The floors were bare—you didn't even get rubber mats. The windows were plastic and slid out. And you opened the door from the inside by pulling on a rope!

Think about that. This is a car with a price tag higher than a luxury house—and it doesn't even have door handles.

But all was quickly forgotten when you stepped on the gas.

The F40's engine was a racing version of the Dino-type V-8. That surprised some Ferrari fans. They'd felt the company's birthday special would be a 12-cylinder machine. But this eight put out more power than any of the 12s. It housed 478 frisky ponies, itching to run free!

Even at that the engine was down on power from what it had when the design was a Group B racer. Ready for the track, it pumped more than 600 horses!

The F40 made Ferrari's other top cars—the Boxers, Daytonas and Testarossas—seem slow. Zero to 60 in those fine cars was in the five-second range. The fantastic F40 rocketed zero to 60 in just 3.5 seconds.

Count out loud to four . . . 1 . . . 2 . . . 3 . . . 4. If you'd been in an F40 you'd now be traveling at the national speed limit.

Its handling also set new records for a road car. But the top praise went to the F40's speed. This was the first nonracing Ferrari able to break the magical 200 mph mark. Top speed was clocked at an amazing 201 mph.

At the time it came out the F40's price was $260,000. And it was still an instant sellout. Its price has since risen to nearly $400,000. Those who've driven an F40 think it's worth every dime.

But not anyone can buy an F40, even if they have the money to do so. The Ferrari company carefully selects buyers. Expert drivers only need apply. If you've bought top-of-the-line Ferraris before, that helps too.

One writer was lucky enough to test the car at Ferrari's own track. "It thrilled me. It scared me," he wrote. "It is the most exciting car I've driven in 35 years."

Another driver put it in a single word. "Unforgettable."

14 THE FUTURE OF FERRARI

Just weeks after Enzo Ferrari showed the F40 to the world, he died quietly at age 90.

In 40 years he'd built only about as many cars as General Motors builds in a week. But from the first 125 S through the F40 almost every one of them had been unforgettable.

The death of Enzo Ferrari did not mean the end of the company. In fact, Enzo had sold part of Ferrari to the Fiat company years before. That meant the company would have a healthy supply of money. Fiat had promised not to try to run things, as Ford had seemed to want to, but to let Ferrari's people do that.

Though Enzo's son Dino had died years before, another son, Piero, was ready to help continue the company in the Ferrari tradition.

He promised that the basic idea of Ferrari would not change. The company would go on building some of the world's most exciting cars.

Since its present leaders have taken over, the Ferrari company has delivered on that promise. There's a hot new design in the V-8 series called the 348, which will probably take Ferrari into the 21st century. Major improvements have been made to the Testarossa, and there are rumors of a new 12-cylinder monster that will take on the latest from Lamborghini and other makers.

To the fire and excitement they've always had, the company's road cars have added a new attention to high-tech details. Today's Ferraris use computer-controlled **fuel injection**. Ferrari has also designed an engine that has four valves per cylinder (that's 48 valves in a Testarossa!). The new engine also allows for freer fuel flow.

The new 348 will probably take Ferrari into the 21st century. It's clean, sleek and high-tech.

Tomorrow's Ferrari may have four-wheel drive, and perhaps four-wheel steering. **Active suspension** is being looked at as well. That's a system in which computers and pumps actively move the wheels of the car up and down to keep control sharp no matter how many bumps or holes are in the road.

The company is also experimenting with new ways to build cars. One experimental Ferrari was put together with a kind of superglue, like a giant model kit. Other makers might not have cared what such a test car looked like, only how it worked.

But Ferrari turned even this test model into a raging yellow roadburner with a high dose of driving excitement.

On the racetrack Ferrari is as active as ever. Success has gone to the British, Germans and Japanese more than to Ferrari in recent years. But that has only seemed to make the Italians try harder. One new racer featured transmission control buttons in the steering wheel. This allowed the driver to shift gears without taking his or her hand—or attention—off the wheel even for a fraction of a second. In big-league racing, where victory has come by finishes 1/100 of a second ahead, that can be a winning edge.

Win or lose—and the company has won between 4,000 and 5,000 races—Ferrari promises always to be on the starting line.

There's a separate department at Maranello that works on racing and only racing. And very few other makers can match their experience in building high-performance engines. It's therefore a safe bet that Ferrari will often be first at the finish line as well.

What keeps the makers of this "cool classic" going? More than 40 years of racing in the blood; the love of thousands of fans; and perhaps the knowledge that, from wherever he is up there, Enzo Ferrari, "Il Commendatore," will always be watching.

GLOSSARY/INDEX

active suspension 45 A computer-controlled system that actively pumps a car's wheels up or down to balance the effect on the car of bumps or holes in the road.

aluminum 14 A lighweight metal.

Barchetta 13, 18 Italian for "little boat," nickname for an early Ferrari.

"Boxer" 34, 36, 43 An engine in which the cylinders and pistons lie in a flat layout. The motion of the pistons is like two prizefighters jabbing away at each other; also the name of a Ferrari high-performance sports coupe with midmounted engine.

composites 42 Lightweight but very strong materials used in building high-performance automobiles and aircraft.

cylinder 11, 34, 43, 44 The empty chamber in which gas is exploded in an engine. The explosion then forces the piston down the cylinder to turn the crankshaft that runs the drivetrain.

designer 29 Creator of a car's appearance and general layout.

disk brakes 17 A stopping system that works by pressing on a spinning disk connected to the wheel. Disk brakes are especially good for stopping in wet weather.

engineer 31 Person who sets out how the car's engine and other parts and systems will work.

fiberglass 31, 42 A plasticlike material used in car bodies. Fiberglass is easy to work with and will not rust. Also used to make skis, crash helmets and other items.

fuel injection 44 System that actively pumps fuel-air mixture into an engine rather than having it drift in. Replaces the carburetor.

GTO 19, 20, 21, 22   Abbreviation for Gran Turismo Omologato. A two passenger "grand touring" sports car approved for both racing and street use; also a famous Ferrari model. The name was also used by Pontiac for one of its models.

Il Commendatore 13, 46   Italian for "The Commander," or "The Boss"; a nickname given to Enzo Ferrari.

NASCAR 22   National Association of Stock Car Auto Racing.

piston 11, 12, 34, 47   The part of an engine moved by the explosion of gasoline and air. The piston moves inside a cylinder and transfers its motion through other parts to turn the wheels.

Scuderia 9   Italian for stable, but also used to mean racing team.

suspension 17   Parts that mount the wheels to a car and allow it to flex up and down with bumps in the road.

Testarossa 37, 38, 43, 44   Italian for "red head," a Ferrari model in which the top parts of the engine, the cylinder "heads," are painted red.

wind tunnel 19, 20   A testing device that blows fast-moving air over a car or aircraft body to check whether anything is blocking smooth flow. Well-designed bodies increase performance while saving energy.